Singing
The Dawn

Poems of Death & Resurrection

by
Caroline Hope

Edited by Jay Ramsay

Caro Publishing
In association with
Chrysalis Poetry

Singing the Dawn

ISBN 978-0-9544918-3-3

Edited by Jay Ramsay

Published by
Caro Publishing
Court Farm House
Little Witcombe
Gloucester
GL3 4TU

In association with
Chrysalis Poetry
5 Oxford Terrace
Uplands
Stroud
Glos. GL5 1TW

Designed by Satori Creative
www.satoricreative.co.uk
Tel: 07515 684306

Printed by
Stroud Print
www.stroudprint.co.uk

Acknowledgements

The Bench – first published in The Sacred Bench, A Collection of Poetry and Paintings, Published by Caro Publishing, 2003, ISBN 0-9544918-0-7.

Tiercel and Tiercel II, Judgement Day, Held in God's Gaze: The Chase, Ghost, Blackbird, November 11th first published in Doorways to the Light, published by Caro Publishing, 2004, ISBN 0-9544918-1-5

November 11th also published in Poetry Church Collection, Winter, 2004, Feather Books.

At Play published in Reckless Hills and Holy Hearts, A Horsley Studio Poet's Anthology, edited by Carolyn Finlay. Published by Chrysalis Poetry, 5 Oxford Terrace, Uplands, Stroud, Glos, GL5 1TW

A Rocky Path published in Gabriel, A Christian Poetry Magazine, Spring, 2009

Special thanks to my Editor, Jay Ramsay (Chrysalis Poetry), Sarah at Satori Creative, and Rev'd David Primrose who listened and encouraged.

Front Cover: North Devon coast at dawn, photograph by the author.
Back Cover: Dawn over Islay, photograph by the author.
Drawings by the author.

Title: "Prose can paint evening and moonlight, but poets are needed to sing the dawn." *George Meredith, Beauchamp's Career*

Preface

Perhaps it's odd that someone as 'unchurched' as myself should be writing Christian-based poems. My religious foundations had deep roots but a pruned and grafted exterior. My mother, a devout member of the Church of England took her family to church every Sunday. Our lives revolved around St Andrew's, Bedford until spells in Africa in teenage years broke the ritual. I have to say, I was a daydreamer; the Sunday School message meant little to me.

By the time I was sixteen I had discovered the mysteries of Yoga, which led me eastwards, spiritually speaking, into the depths of the Upanishads, the Bhagavad Gita, and on to touching Buddhism, The Study Society, Bede Griffiths and Krishnamurti. Feelers also went back to parallels with Christianity. It was a rich time of deep awareness which had been sparked, at age 18 by a lonely journey into unknown territory, when I had, at the same time, been stripped of my secure home base. It was indeed my equal to a trip into the unknown 'desert,' which had started me looking at myself deeply. Even so, perhaps I had not processed the painful episode sufficiently but it remained stored up in my psyche through a long secular period in which the suffering-stuff of life accumulated further. Shakyamuni Buddha summed it up succinctly: the pain of birth, the loneliness of old age, the anxiety of sickness, the fear of death; added to which is the loss of those we love through illness, through death; dealing with desire; understanding illusory thinking and finding out that all this 'suffering' happens in the vessel of our bodies. I would like to point out here that suffering is not the prerogative of the poor and needy. Suffering affects us all. We seek its meaning and look for help in shouldering the burden, otherwise it so easily may mould us into victims consumed by resentment.

The Buddha's teaching went east. Coming west 500 years later, it was Jesus Christ who showed us another way through the self-same sufferings of life by looking into the spiritual nature of ourselves; finding something more permanent than these bodies of ours. We find our life reflected in Him and if we look deep enough, his nature patterned in us. But there always seems to be this painful separation – we project our Christhood outside ourselves onto Jesus 2,000+ years ago. There we leave him, the still calm centre of love, peace, wisdom and understanding, kept forever snagged on nails on a hillside outside Jerusalem. How can we - I - make this relevant to me, here and now? How can I understand what is meant by "He died for our sins?" *(Root and Flower, p46).*

This is how my second years-long desert experience ended; with a choice – an invitation *(The Bench, p3)*, which turned into an insistence, *(Tiercel, p4* and *The Chase, p6)* to revisit my spiritual grounding and to move on from this, or stay back in the secular wilderness. Moving on meant the many years spent in the desert had to be addressed. Yes, there had been pain, loss, anxiety and death – and, yes, I had been obliged to take a look at my own mortality *(In the Footsteps of the Magi, p17)*. These things leave their marks and I have sought, in these poems, to come to an understanding of the Christian spiritual message, not, as it happened 2000+ years ago and its subsequent appropriation, but in me, here and now, a body living in a modern world of rapid change and upheaval. And then looking beyond piety to realize that we are all capable of every atrocity – we are all culpable in our separateness. *(As Easter Approaches, p42)*.

What a joy to discover that these three great religions which have shaped my soul, so different in cultural expression on the surface of things, have at their heart the same message and cause – the evolution of the human spirit by the love of God to a higher consciousness – the Christ consciousness, the Buddha nature, Krishna the light. And can we live it, this interfaith? As Thomas Merton asked, can we live it, flesh and blood, not just talk piously about our tolerant attitude; can we step beyond creeds and dogma into humility, truth and presence? *(The Chase, p6* and *Three Wise Men, p19)*. It's a tall order!

I stand on the bridge, in suspension
between east and west, heaven and earth,
heaven and the hell of my closed heart,
letting go of desire by this Christian yoga
and yoking instead to God.

Stepping up into the greater grace of Christ
dancing, like Shiva, on the eggshell of the ego.

Finding a Way
for the great creative spirit of Christ
to live on in art,
in poetry.

Caroline Hope, March 2011

Foreword

Living with her family on a farm in Gloucestershire, Caroline is embedded within her local community, editing the village magazine, running the annual pantomime. She is an acute observer of all around her, from the dynamic beauty of the earth to the colourful characters of the surrounding neighbourhood. What she sees so clearly in her environs is in constant dialogue with what she sees within. She was already an accomplished artist when, as her vicar, we met in the late-90s. During breaks from painting, she has revisited poetry, with ever increasing effectiveness. The soft mystery of paint blending colour, shape and texture is succinctly expressed in the written word, sometimes playful, always evocative. The same creative spirit guides both brush and pen.

Caroline is wary of dogma, instinctively protesting whenever definition threatens inclusivity. She knows that when the ego is dominant, the strong and powerful assert a monopoly on freedom *(Three Wise Men, p19)*. From a religious perspective, eastern enlightenment taught her an openness with which she looks back into the western church to portray Christ in graphic yet enigmatic vulnerability *(I am going from you now, p54* and *Emmaus, p48)*.

Spanning a decade, these poems articulate inner truths through a perceptive interplay with the natural world around us. They are divided into four thematic sections. In the first collection, the potency of the encounter is explored by baptism *(Lost Moments, p7)*; by death *(November 11th, p12* and *The Field, p13)*; and by birth *(Christmas and New Year poems)*. Then we move on to the metaphor of journey, where the destination shares meaning with the immediate *(Mystery, p33* and *At St Bueno's Rock, p35)*. In Touching the Wound, inhabiting suffering is the beginning of redemption *(A Lesson in Washing Feet, p43* and *Doubting Thomas, p51)*. In the end, life triumphs as expressed by the joy of *The Blackbird* and *The Lark* and a return to the first elemental meeting place *(Water, page 75)*.

Enjoy, read, listen and be blessed by these manifestations of hope.

Rev'd David Primrose, Spring, 2011

Something infinite,
older than heaven and earth,
silent, solitary, and vast;
eternal, unchanging,
yet ever evolving
throughout ten thousand things.
Not knowing its name
I call it Tao.

Lao Tzu

Thine be the kingdom, power and the glory
forever and ever;
ever evolving ever loving.
Not knowing its name
I call it God.

To embrace all things
means that one rids oneself
of any concept of separation:
male and female,
self and other, life and death.
Division is contrary
to the nature of Tao.

Lao Tzu

To respond with compassion
not as Christian to some poor 'other'
but as being human
to human being

Contents

MEETING

PILGRIM

TOUCHING THE WOUND

RENEWAL

MEETING

The bench

We share the bench;
the bench
at the beginning of the end
or the end of the beginning;

the way we came
solid earth manifest;

The way we go
sea and sky infinite;

"Either come with me
or go back," he said.

Tiercel

In his stillness the Tiercel hangs
attendant on the moment,
attuned to the raging gale buffet,
which is of inconsequence
to his peace within.

For from his immobility
he casts his eye over the green pasture
and it is fixed on me.

I have run. I have hidden,
but each time he slices the wind
and remains above
in his stillness, in his solitude.

His cry is taken from his belly to his throat
and is caught in the elemental roar.
It pierces and I am frozen.

He descends.
The light falls to earth
in vertical arrow shaft.
I am caught in his shadow
for I no longer see the worldly sun.

And in the agony of surrender
his angelic wings
enfold me in mantling protection.
He breathes,
"Fear not. For I am with you,
here in your heart,
here in the hearts of all.
I am."

And in the consuming fire
we become one.
And in the singularity
I am carried aloft in his grip,
fearless, to the heavens.

Tiercel II

Carried aloft in our singularity
the Tiercel uttered soft love sounds
in my soul.
I was just to be;
and now, am consumed.

This is my goal! I am food for God!
This is His need; this is how He grows.
I have to concede, my holy task was acceptance
of His love. In consumption I am to become His Essence,
and am to live on in other silent souls,
healing tired spirits, turning heads
to face the Tiercel,
to face righteousness.
God's work will be done.

Then joyously let it come to me when the time is right!
for I am ready now and expectant for that last journey to the light.

*The Tiercel is the male falcon and takes its inspiration from
Gerard Manly Hopkin's poem, The Windhover, To Christ Our Lord.*

Held in God's gaze: The chase

Who ran through my dream?
A sea of silver seeded globes
scattering heads floating airborne
in the wake of fleeting feet.
Where was that happiness running to?
Up, up and away.

Making chase, coursing, wild eyed,
not seeing wood for trees
he leaves me tumbled out
at God's feet; he flees.

I am trapped in that fearful unknowing space
to feel, in my heaving breath,
His Presence.

He is as still as stone;
holding me, hare-like,
in servient thrall;
I do not speak, only await his call;
filled with desire to know,
I dare not look on His face,
yet I dare not go.

My graven God,
cold in remote awesome splendour,
comes alive when I,
in unknowing Trust, surrender.

I reach up,
a humble spirit
chastening all adult pride.
He lifts the child;
holds the baby to His breast;
but it is in newborn form
that my helpless quest
melts His heart.
Mine melts in His;
we shall not part.

Lost moments

He took hold of me
- by the scruff of the neck -
and dangled me over the edge.
I screamed, recoiled,
from the fathomless fear,
the unknown depth of his presence,

My toes touched the truth.
It was warm.
I scanned the horizon for a white flag.

"Look," he said, twisting my ear
until my face turned to the Ocean below,
"look at all those unrecognised moments."

I had thought it was me in them, not Him.

Limp now,
I trust his gentler hold, as,
with care, he lowers me feet first.

Then knees, legs, hips,
stomach, chest,
arms stretched horizon wide,
shoulders, neck,
face, eyes closing,
head.
All is submerged

dipped, like an apple into toffee.

Emerging,
coated in love.

The Artist and the Art

She is being painted.

She looks behind and sees only ancient frescos,
their colours flaking on the walls of history;
and up ahead, a blank canvas,
white and untouched.

The brush moves her;
paints her colour
paints her with delight.

She turns in one stroke to gaze
into the moment of her creation;
into her never ending resurrection
and feel, fleetingly,
the power that moves the brush.

The Old Master paints her now,
as He painted all those faded scenes gone before
with their thoughts locked under
cracked and yellowing varnish;
as He will paint all the thought now wasted
on hasty charcoal possibilities
smudged by time.

But it is only *now* that His spirit gleams in her eyes;
now, when her attention is trapped in the light,
the vibrant colour still wet with living water;
the form etched in the presence of her Creator's love.

He gazes at her beauty and purity
in silence.
He cherishes her without lust,
without desire.
She is exposed in His holding,
safe in His love.

As the paint dries
He opens a new page...

Sketchbooks
(for Maxine)

Sketchbook legacies
holding so many memories
capturing lost moments
imprisoning some sort of permanence
in a creation that will not wait

and while the transcendent nebulae of our lives
travel in light
streaming at God's speed to infinity
these spiral bound life-times
are entrapped like prayers
immortalised on paper
hastily brushed moments of light and dark
recalling the beauty of incarnation
and leaving them immanent in the world

the world of never-knowing
of living with death on our shoulders
of wondering in our impoverished imaginations

how do we become willing to let go?

Living Waters

It is as if
when we meet
beside the well
there is you
there is me
and between us
the dark depth
of the well.

We are able
to dip
beyond causation
into the source
drawing forth
cups of love.

We slake
our yearning,
drinking deeply
from the cup
at once held to your lips
at once held to mine

this cup of love
this cup of light
this cup
of the Divine.

The well

There is music
in the faint depths of the well.

In silence
the distant echo floats

I
am
light
I am
the peace
of the world.

I am light
I am the peace
of the world.

I am light
I am the peace of the world.

The light
always sings in the abyss

a song
released in your soul.

"I am light I am the peace of the world" from Om Shanti
from A Hundred Thousand Angels by Bliss

November 11ᵗʰ

Whispers of death
in an autumn sacrifice of golden falling
and jumbling one above the other;
bronze hewn, red bloodied
or parchment yellow, rotting, skeletal;
faint breathing spirits
in their last gasp.

Each year the memory feeds the next,
the trapped ancient sunlight
releasing back into renewal.
For when the light glints
on the sacrificial death pile
a glory is witnessed;
A shining powerful glory
seen in the woods, in the fields,
under trees, smothering the sun blest earth.

Speak to these soldiers through the ethereal tracery
of their passing,
a ghostly mist absorbing the words...
The dying whisper comes back,
"We, too, were blessed,
for we lie in peace
wrapped in this cloth of gold."

The field

The field is littered with the dead.

So many lie together,
tossed and heaped in a cheapened aggregate
of corporeal form,
a multitude of mixed race muffled
dormant dead.

They cannot face
the cold soul of winter's night
and choose instead
to rot where they fall,
carrion food, pulled into earth
by worms in a pall
of heavy sorrow,
grieving for the year gone by

these leaves which heave
a mournful sigh
and await a new tomorrow.

A Christmas Mystery

I am caught in a mystery
as dark and brittle as a Christmas night
crystallised by crisp moon beams
shining their silver light
on flinted furrowed fields.

In the night watch hour
Christ Light is as ether,
like iced starlight
shining ghostly on frost-bitten rattling thoughts
which are swallowed in the void of His enigma.

This Unknowing is
cluttered by the crust of creation,
which seems as ephemeral
as the surface tension of a tear drop,
jerking its reflected highlights
painfully across a heavy laden and vulnerable cheek
to melt in His engulfing ocean of Love.

I am caught in a mystery,
a Christmas joy,
which shows me only that which I need to see.
For in cherishing the depths of His naked infant soul
He shows me nothing of the shell of Himself,
only the hidden depths of me.

Midnight at St Mary's

Shards of moonlight, cold as iced confetti,
mosaic the lonely lych.
The split of atomised breath
and inhale of scalpel sharp anticipation.
The shadowed murmur of dim sighted faces
as bracing step silent footfall
blitz the dark as pitch lane.

A keen clamour of St Mary's church bell
tumble in calling from the glooming vespertine tower
breaking open the crystal bright midnight hour
frosty with a million glinting stars
clear twinkling in dome dark witching sky.

Entering surrounded by air zest,
ebullient smiles in greeting
and inside candle lit soft, golden warmth
snugly lapped and flickering
kindling a winter glad, scarf wrapped, joy trapped Christmas.

The dawn, a monochrome moment of black and white,
a slept through silent coming,
awakens sleepily to the rising of the Light.

Festive Season

The world roars and hums
in a congestion of motorway, car,
lorry, body, ebb and flow,

on a mission to shop till we drop,
for tinsel and wine, bauble and cracker
tempting our time a while away;

empty, empty it flows away
another year, another day;
another failing to find the promised peace
in such ephemeral Christmas cheer and beer,
such frantic wrappings and trappings,
festive greetings and dutiful meetings

as the silent spirit breezes, un-noticed, by;

It is gone, gone; gone beyond
to the still and peaceful solstice hill
where dead grasses whisper
and bare trees sigh:

gate,
gate,
pare gate,
pare sam gate,
bodhi svaha . . .

Hail to thee enlightened one*

*Heart Sutra

16

In the footsteps of the Magi
with thanks to TS Eliott

But set this down –
SET THIS DOWN –
I had travelled far
ignited by a light of hope
a light that illumined the mind,
showed the way,
revealing truth – calling me home.

Set this down:
it was a wilderness I struggled through.
I lost everything in that desert, bit by bit:
pride, selfishness, sorrow, stupidity –
all those tears shed
the many swords pulled from the heart –
rejection, abandonment, fear, loss,
memories of good times, bad times when
I had shuddered in the face of death.
All these things were discarded along the way
and then I travelled unburdened
following a point of light in the darkness.

And the journey ended in poverty,
humility, blessedness – a quiet place –
out of the way of the world's madness.
and I found purity there
and in her womb
was new life created by
a rising spirit of love.

What little I had I gave – treasure to me –
matchless though, to the pearl I had found,
and a knowing that in this new way
the old me had died.

A death, yes, certainly there was a death.

Set this down:
I had been crucified in some small way,
felt the all too real wounds
inflicted by the world
and risen on Christ's healing wings.
I too returned a stranger, ill at ease
in a world of untruth.
But I would do it again
and again –
as often as it is willed necessary.

Three Wise Men

Who are these Magi,
figure-flinging Shamen on a quest for self,
riding out of the cold desert
seeking transformation,
hope like a star in their hearts?

They pass out of Herod's ego state,
a land fallen into three temptations,
poisoned by envy and sick with hate,
a country fearing obscurity, hunger, death.

Stripped of kingly pride our three Alchemists
ride out of the wilderness
to a place of humility,
a silent place,
a place of grace.
And in this hidden room
rich with joy
they find what they
did not know they sought,
a new birthing,
an innocence whose tiny form
embodied infinite spirit.

Ahh, such treasures they bring
in their wondering breasts,
such offerings spilling out of their open hearts
as they kneel on holy humble ground
between the cow's warm breath and the lamb's bleat,
the shepherd's crook and the donkey's gentle feet.

Here they are transformed by their own obscure deaths,
dissolved and reformed
in the fire of burning gold, myrrh and frankincense.

And I stood at the gate of the year,★
a pilgrim facing an unknown home.

Behind, in my journey,
the winter-antlered forest,
a memory now,
her dark stillness
waiting;

and crowding up behind my feet,
her shroud of fallen leaves;
once rich colours fading
on their bare-boned frames.

I stand at the edge of the year,
the trees patiently attentive,
nudging me forward
into wide open spaces
where there are no boundaries
no landmarks
no restrictions or limitation
no shadows

just a fearless light

and all that I now see
already lives in me.

★This line is from the poem *The Gate of the Year,* which commences,
  "I said to the man who stood at the gate of the year"
  by Minnie Louise Haskins, 1908

At the turn of the Year

We awoke, that morning
to a silenced world.
A sleeping standstill of
white silence.
It was smothering the Severn Vale
in a heavy, palling atmosphere
of snow.

May Hill was just visible;
a familiarity in the distant peace,
as we struggled up the slope,
sledges primed for joyful descent.

We, breathing a solstice breath,
and more of us, one by one,
bringing colour,
finding delight
in the zest
of the mysterious midwinter air;
expectant
in this still point around which the season wheels
and reveals a rebirth
a new coming of light.

Pilgrim

A stroll in the garden

I suggested to my Beloved Friend
that He take a stroll
in His garden
to savour the perfume
of all the spring blossom
whose essence was suspended
in the soft fragrant sunshine.

He asked me
how was He to do that?

I took Him by the hand.

Lion

There are times
it seems like a tiny seed has come to lodge
in the warm soil of my heart.

The expansion
forces the earth to part
and explosively, from the centre,
He leaps, roaring, into sunlight.

It would be hard to pass through
His golden needled eyes
which are narrowed
against the unfamiliar heat haze,
but He turns to look back,
without menace,
to my innocence.

With sheathed paws
He hangs His coat over my shoulders,
the glorious sunsilked mane
rippling against my cheek;
a rumble of allegiance purring from His throat.

Message

'Between the idea and the reality
falls the shadow'
and out of the shadow
a hand
always outstretched, the arm
stretched out, across infinity
and broken through a thin moment,
a crack in time, called presence.

And in the warm idea,
like a princess caught in the night,
I reach out; always reaching out,
forever taking the waiting hand,
constantly accepting,
opening and receiving
in the has been,
the now and shall be
of the world without end.

And the royal emergence,
the stepping up and out,
endlessly repeated,
the falling away of shadow
revealing the simple dress of purity.

'Between the idea and reality, the shadow'
now falling away,
as stepping up and into His eyes,
knowing all we have to do is get
The Message.
And the message in His eyes
is love.

A rocky path
(for Jenny)

I see you
cliff hanging over the emotional abyss.

Fellow man, I've been there –
not known how to show,
or flow in motion;
caught inside a dark universe.
I too trapped God in hermetic stone.
I've been pinned to the secular cross:
forsaken
poked and prodded by the unreal world
hardened the pain and grief
looked at death.

I've been there, traveller,
in your boots.
I've trod that path,
kicked those rocks.

Pilgrim, how can I help you on your way?
To loosen your laces?
Enable you to
step out onto the verdant pasture?
The soft grass under your soul,
the hill rising up to meet you
at a place above
where, barefoot and unafraid
you will stand . . .

a star in your heart.

And, like cherry blossom drifting
from wet-blackened branches
words will fall,
clustering at your fingertips,
filling your lips,
willing you, dear poet
to make them real.

Journey into Wilderness
(for Bishop Declan Lang)

The wilderness is silent
barren, poor
and in it the voiceless scream –

a shuddering fear of destitution
as it hurtles towards you
tearing body from soul,

and passes, leaving
only a still small humility
a new and different emptiness

a rich poverty.

The seduction is in your surrender
not to imprisonment from the world
but a willingness to be shackled,
hand and foot,

to the chains of freedom.

Finding it is surrender
to God's law of love.

East of Eden

It's a different country of fierce landscapes
of blazing heat and numbing cold
where man travels and travails alone.

Was this Eden business a sort of reverse psychology?
That wily old
God of old
would know that a "Thou shalt not,"
would engender a "But I shall and will!"
knowing that it *would* lead us into temptation.
(Oh Lord, forgive us, lead us not into that place).

Yes, I think He wanted it
and then to touch us with holy spirit
to remind us of homeland.
How else would His love live and endure
But out here in a world of dualities?

And, like children, we have been screaming
to get our own way;
kicking against the traces of consciousness
whilst the patient parent waited, waits,
feeding us with creativity,
wanting us to excel,
hoping for the Glory to hit us.

Have we really fallen by the wayside
or are we growing still?
feeling our way, finding gifts
of love and inspiration mysteriously,
outrageously given –
living from the increase,
building God's garden.

It comes with maturity,
the wisdom and compassion
that is not of our own engendering
that is given back, always, to Him.

We find the father, once so severe
in His limitations upon us
now loving and benevolent towards his trusting children.
We find our minds now open to unlimited possibility.

And, in the torment of our physicality,
fully aware of our nakedness,
we stand on holy ground
as God strips us of our self-sown garments,
our cover-ups, excuses, all our babbling words
and clothes us, instead, with light.

Judgement Day *(Do not squander your life)*

When the day comes
that you are asked
how you spent your time,
will your answer be
that your life was a day dream,
your reality uncertain,
your comfort make believe,
your thoughts a distraction?
Or will your answer be
that you spent your life
in loving remembrance,
attending every impulse,
every sacred second;
that all the world was a reminder
to stay in this place, in reverence;
not one second lost,
not one second wasted?

Will you also wonder
does madness come?
The mind reeling in blank unknowing,
the only thought being
I don't know who I am any more.
There is only desperation for memory – any memory,
for it was easier to live in daydreams, than this liberty.

Walking in stillness,
the trees' omnipresence in silent
command of respect,
namaste they whisper,
as the breeze
takes their leaves
to remind, to remind me.

When I don't know who I am anymore,
when I feel the worldly flood of rage,
I listen to the trees, the living sacred trees,
and know that this bird needs a cage.

Mystery

"Look at the mystery,"
he said
and the lime avenue drifts away
in smudges of blue,
purple and grey.

"Where is the end?" I ask.
"What is the end?"

"Wait for the enlightenment,"
he said.

I wait
on the bench
watching the oppressive clouds crowding the sky,
looking for blue
looking for heaven,
looking for the gap in my thought.

"The light is coming," he said.
"Wait."

And its glory
suddenly bursting through the trees
flooding and flushing
the unknown from its hiding place
illuminating
each tree along the way,
dissolving and disappearing
all mystery from the
shadowed confusion.

"Here, at the end,"
he said,
"is clarity."

The Gift

The old covering had
slipped to the ground unnoticed.
It lay on the forest floor
forgotten,   .
withdrawn into
frozen moments of inaction.

And then the invitation
to go deeper in,
to enter curiosity,

and out of nowhere
held by no one
a velvet cushion –
on it, there's a kinda hush
a hush and a rush of silence.

I take it,
the corner,
shake it out, flaunt
the rippling, silky silence
wrap it round, spinning jauntily
colours melding, merging
fluttering behind me ...

and then the silence broke, spoke saying,
"Can you no longer watch with me one hour,
not even one minute of your day?"

A falling cloak of stillness
settles guiltily around me
gift wrapping me
with quiet charity,
piercing my forgetfulness.

At St Bueno's Rock with Gerard Manly Hopkins

I hold in my hand the chapel key.
Is this the key leading me
to truth?
It's an early morning dew wet walking,
tall grasses spindle stalking,
high wind in lofty summer trees,
these trees speaking, branches creaking.

All things *are* dappled, moving
twisting, countered, bright,
                dark leaved, light
and the screaming wire wind slicing tight;
blush a bluster, shaken, stirred
and no one here to hear, not a word
to disturb the shaking,
                quaking, torn up trees.

I am alone and bold, monk-cowled against the cold
in monastery silence
                alone here on the rock
                atone here on the rock
                at one here on the rock.

A Bible and celtic cross, candle,
incense ash, the arrow-window eastern light
                sunlit slash;
a prayer stool for a Zen praying fool.

This is a thin place; thin for Him.
I come for Him to draw me in.
I am prey, preyed on, my own heart,
like Hopkin's gashed and burnt
                coals, *gold vermillion*★ splash.

The Bible is waiting,
                left open it seems;
"Know ye not, ye are gods?"

I stand on holy ground.

"Know ye not, ye are gods?"
Teach me, good Lord, all I fear to be so.
"Ye are gods,"
        bright stars, *immortal diamonds.*★★

And the glory of God here unfolds,
each breath, each breathing spirit
in outline gold leaf bound
in the window light I am found.

★from Gerard Manly Hopkins, *Windhover – To Christ Our Lord*
★★from Gerard Manly Hopkins, *That nature is a Heraclitean Fire and of the comfort of the Resurrection*

A silent meditation in Gloucester Cathedral

Marbled breath cold
plinth-pressed flesh
breath and flesh etched in rock
tied to bone.

Hollowed out whispers
fanned and vaulted echoes
stone-stained
the wind paned
flies by buttress
flows over
the foot-of-monk worn
doorway stone
in silent moan.

Each whispering prayer ascending
by spiral stair
reverberant in cathedral dome

escaping to firmament magnifying
the unforgotten memory of home
and re-found in the
earth bound
cloistered round
ambulatory soul
sound

TOUCHING
THE WOUND

Easter Egg

'Each moment is like an Easter Egg,' He said,
'whole and complete
incubating its gift.'

'Each unknown moment an Easter Egg,' He said,
'containing the yolk,
a tantalizing expectancy
awaiting your full term relish.'

'Each moment is an Easter Egg,' He said,
'waiting to be cracked open;
and inside –
a mouth full of eternity,
the dark centre of Divinity.'

As Easter approaches

I find, I am culpable
and shallow in compassion;
as fickle fenced and capable
of both crucifixion and silent sorrow.
I am locked in that prison of inability
to speak up and say, "Enough!"

What is it I fear?

The horror is recognising that I can be
all these, so easily:
accuser, abuser, grieving mourner,
even betrayer
and, too, she who denies by turning away
from the things men do.

For how often do I crucify?
How often am I crucified?
How often do I dare stand up
and cry out for truth?

My heart is in fragments

but from this desert
Christ lifts me
and I watch with him
as he forgives.

A lesson in washing feet

He stopped me
as I walked in the garden
cloistered against the cold.

"Are you in resistance
To this Now?"
He said,
"this moment of glory?

Come,
let God wash your feet,
let yourself be embraced
by the Maundy morning chill."

I am recollected
to the repose
which is faltering still
in the quiet shadow
of winter's death

and to the
flickering movement
of the breezy daffodils'
sunlit yellow intensity,
trumpeting,
"Wake up, look at me!"

"Let God wash your feet
in this hallowedness,"
He said.
Ah . . .
that He should do this
every day, every moment

for me.

A little crucifixion

Just a little crucifixion
the cold nail breaking the veil of skin

she bleeds

the indifferent nail
piercing flesh

she bleeds

the incurious nail
fixing her pinions to the wood

she bleeds

and then the sword,
fearful of her love,
plunging into the soul
bringing tears to her uncomprehending eyes,
dark with grief.

And the abundant bread and wine
which she had brought back from her flight
being returned with a bitter pill to her lips.

It had been a blessing, a privilege;
to be given the chance
to endure,
to love him still

so that

three days later
she walks
free.

Death and Resurrection

Entering the cold church
cold, like a tomb,
with a silence so heavy
it drips from the walls
oozing sweat and blood
form its porous stone.

Separate from the vacuous body.
Separate from the fullness of God.

Waiting
waiting in the hushing stillness
waiting in the staining light.

The door latch splitting the silence
awakening the echoes of death
putting asunder the heinous door
which guards
the embalming of ignorance.

Root and Flower

Did you do this for me?
Am I root, so solid earth
or flower, fragility of all humanity?
Or is it the life force flowing in the stem
feeding me, root to flower?

and the ecstasy of knowing I belong somehow to you.

Did you really die for *me?*
I didn't ask for it.
You could have saved your own skin
and lived out your life, an outcast,
deep in your own personal prayer.

But when even stepping out of the boat was not sufficient,
I guess you had to die
or I
and all people who walked then and walk now in darkness
would be forever trapped in slavery to the loveless
by a hundred oughts and shoulds;
thou shalts and thou shalt nots;
veils, burkhas and Sabbath-keeping circumcisions.

But you could not leave it that way
for your death loosed the universal soul
out of the security of the boat of religious belief
into the freedom of God.

And if I should keep your humanity
always suffering, snagged on nails,
it is to remember your gift of truth:
the precious release from the oppression
of other people's thought, belief and egoic greed
which live a death in history.

Your Easter gift is this:
the eternal luminous pearl
of knowing
(what I was too blind to see)
that here I am
grown in your great light
flower *and* root,
a being
of one substance
with you.

Emmaus

And when
our perceptions
have stripped this
beloved
Christ

of all his beguiling attractiveness, and reduced him to a stranger on the road;
and the singularity, so hard to recognise, purposes his disappearance

from our lives, we find
in our grieving at the loss
of our cherished
separation from him
there is the deeper
knowledge of the
eternal atonement.

But how do we let go
of the embalmed
dreams and hungers
that hold us back
like empty shells
in the desert of
this world?

I sit
on the bench
alone and
at one
for
he has

gone

and
the light dances

dances in the
autumn trees
dances in the
heart of me

The mystical gardener

When love came looking
she did not recognise Him
waiting in the garden half light
waiting in the seam between
misty dawn and clear blue sky of morning;

the enlightenment ripping apart
this delicate join between heaven and earth
for

when love came looking
failing to find that beloved corporeal form
instead turning in on her own stricken heart
finding therein her Christ; risen;
too close to touch, too close for recognition.

When love came looking
grieving and hungry for love
meeting disarmed and vulnerable
in the crumbling night;
feeding on love,
consumed by love,
surrendered to love

and God,
being rooted in her garden that morning,
was nourished and grew
by the rapturous consummation.

What is Truth?

We seek the truth
and answers don't come that easily
      distracted by the chop and change of our lives
      disowning the still and silent interior.

Great thinkers, caught in the fleshy flotsam,
have more to say on the matter;
      that truth is relevant;
      different for everybody
but in the deepest depth of things
can the truth be other than what is the same for all –
      the still calm centre around which all things turn
      the still calm centre of Christ?

We seek the supreme reality of ourselves
and look to Jesus, 'our childhood's pattern,'
patterning our lives on him.
How can we respond but with silence also –
His innocent, defenceless silence;
a willingness not to know on the glittering surface
of things but to cherish the answer held close in our womb;
an intrinsic unchanging truth –

eternity incarnating
as life,
living now as you, as me,
together as new wine,
in Christ;
patterned.

Doubting Thomas

Thomas, where are you?
    In me, doubting redemption,
    turned away, buried in a tomb of pain.

Thomas, give me your hand.
    Placing the fingers in the wound,
    feeling around the raw edges of the hurt
    and the suffering of life.

The touch making it real,
drawing it into the light.

The light changing history, changing pain.
The release, a resurrection, stripped of self;
a rising, bearing only the stigma of a wounded life
no longer suffering its pain.

Christ.

Thomas, come out from your tomb,
touch your wound, live and be alive
by this greater grace given.

Moving on

The old construct is no longer lived in,
soul sloughed like a shard of skin,
the shed reduced to ashes.

A moment's pause as she dips her finger
into the soft grey powder
and marking a cross on her forehead
raises her eyes from the dead weight of decay.

The new build seems to contain
the blue jewel of heaven,
filling the interior space,
flooding from the windows –
a sapphire fitting her palm;

pocketed
in Lent she waits

The Cross

We stand, broken, like a scarecrow,
arms outstretched,
crossed at the heartwood,
feet rock rooted,
head heavenly held,
bringing God to earth,
liberating God to world.

I am going from you now

In St Asaph's a skeletal Christ hangs,
bone and sinew, wood and iron made,
flesh gone, a corpse rotted from,
shards of skin varnished thin,
thorny crown, head hung down.

A man, yes, vulnerable and tender,
once flesh and blood.
I dreamt that I held him,
this Christ, this fleshed out man.
I clung to him as he wasted free
from my anguished grasp,
his thin, fluid flesh
slipping through my fingers,
the fire in his belly
smouldered out,

smouldering on in me.

The Naked Christ: a sculpture by
Michele Coxonin St Asaph's Cathedral, North Wales.

A Grief

This is my deepest grief, plaguing the root of my soul;
the denial of the truth of myself.

By crucifying Christhood over and over
I turn away from immortality,
burying myself in the world.

I dance around what is too much to bear
with emotionalism, business or
blissful expressions, acting out piety

but always this dull divine ache of grief
brings me back, keeps me rooted.

A Friend in God
For Bishop Michael

It's a tall order —
making friends with the unknowable, the eternal infinite,
cradling this mystery in our self and all people,
dying to our neighbour and then in the risen humility,
(for what else is left when we shed our self-seeking conceit?)
kneeling, bare-armed, before the pilgrim
taking the broken shoes from the wanderer's feet
bathing the blistering sores
peeling the skin carefully apart between the festering toes
allowing him to walk cared-for footsteps once more.

We eat from the same bowl,
rich man, poor man, beggar man, thief,
drink from the same divine cup.

Second Coming

You could wait forever
on a cold and draughty street corner
for the Kingdom of Heaven to turn up
and give you a lift;
braving the winter wind,
looking for shelter,
expectant that Jesus will be there,
just around the corner,
strolling towards you,
a haven calming the storm –
you would be his first disciple,
second time round.

You could wait forever for that future.

Come out of the cold, go home my friend.
Is he not there, sitting at the table eating with you,
so close you don't recognise the face he wears?
Putting the law of love in your heart,
the word of God in your mouth.
Why else did he leave you, flesh and blood,
if not for you to find Him,
here and now, at home in you,
stamped with His divinity.

RENEWAL

Ghost

The butterfly child
waits daily at this quiet corner
driven from the road hell
where she no longer belongs.

She lives on a wing and a prayer
caught in the moment,
behind time –
a painted lady
hoping for release,
an unfolding from
the encasing chrysalis.
Waiting for rebirth
her living to end.

Blackbird

When the blackbird sang
it was as if
God had opened the throat
and made a portal
through which He could float,
the most sublime of sounds,
the sweetest note.

Astonished, the bird fell silent
and closed his throat
and looked about with listening ear
unknowing it was himself
who raised the presence here,
himself the conduit for the heavenly song,
coming straight from Source,
a place where we all belong.

The Lark

There's a lark alarming
high in the sky,
its cascading song in praising
an upward and descending flight,
returning its glory to the light.

There's a lark ascending
a stairway to love
on feathery gossamers of air uprising
and trembling its voice from heaven above
in spirals, trilling, spilling back to earth
and heard by ears which hear
that which we already know.

Through our hollowness
the praising strain is streaming
straight back for immortal gain.

The Word

They crumbled around me
the words of the poem
the words of the prayer
the words of the priest
the revelation
the breaking of truth.

The given bread
the fallen crumb
the gathered seed
taken eaten
united become.

It crumbled around me
the word
the breaking of truth.

Cocoon

In a cocoon of silence
transforming
base
to gold,

angelic wings
unfold
emerging
coated in love

to taste
nectar.

God's breath
turns stone
to loving heart
blowing gently
and touching soft lips
on the cold sea smoothed crystal
healing
your memory.

Youarechrist

I was asked what I was doing
sitting on the hillside
wrapped in a blanket.

I replied,
"Taking communion from God
of course.

Isn't it obvious?'

Umbrella

I have long taken shelter
from dangerous downpours
under an umbrella
but now
as I close the umbrella
I find I am in a shower
of blessings.

They rain down on me,
sent by the beloved;
sheets of grace
drops of peace
shards of light
mists of love.

I turn my face up to
these blessings.
They soak me in life.

At Play

In the lambent space beyond the graveyard,
across the valley of the shadow of death,
children's voices beckon.

They fear no evil in laughter,
by their calling to one another in play;

their footballs comfort them
in the playing fields of self-forgetfulness.

In the still waters of my heart
can I rediscover a sunlit green pasture
where I may run
and run
spinning in the same boundless joy?

An evensong meadow where my mouth will be opened
and I shall sing
and sing
my belly-to-throat fearless earth shattering song?

Intimate

She stepped out
into a morning freshly arisen
from the shock
of the first October frost

and felt God's breath on her face.

She told him,
"I feel Your cool breeze on my cheek."

He asked,
"What does it feel like?"

She had not realized
He did not know,
could not know.

She described to Him wordlessly
of its coolness, its gentleness;
how its caressing tendrils whispered on her skin
and how it trickled out of the autumn stillness
bringing His presence to all it touched
with a faint rustle,
a flicker of light,
the tumbling of golden leaves,
the scent of change.

Weeping, she told Him,
"It's beautiful."

"Ahh," He sighed,
"good."

Intimate II

She stepped out and said to God,
"I have a cancer deep in my body."

He asked,
"What does it feel like?"

"God, it's a bugger.
The treatment left me broken
and now it has spread all over.
It feels like hell."

"Ahh," said God, dispassionately.
"Do you see that cherry blossom?
Do you feel the cool autumn breeze on your cheek?"

"Yes," she said.

"What does it feel like?" He asked.

"It is so beautiful," she said.

"Hold on to that truth," God answered.

Birdcage

Waiting in a pastoral scene,
he traps her in his eye,
transferring the vision to canvas,
then drawing her to the mountain top,
where, imprisoned in his cage of patience
he gilds her wings with light;
paints the colours of love in her heart;
teaches her the song
which waits unsung in her soul.

She is ringed, identified,
released from the image
and, fingers linked,
he waits for her to sing,
ascending in his eye
like the lark,
like two sky larks
on sun bright wings

feathered tip to tip
vanishing in a body of light
vanishing in upward flight.

Golden Light

I am here
a golden gateway flooding with golden light

as narrow as a needle's eye
and on the other side too
I am here
in this crease of light
which folds
and hems around us all

We are where the edges meet
as the horizon's insubstantial pinning

where earth is tacked to sky
where oceans merge with atmosphere
where the golden fire sinks through the seam

held together by
golden threads of light

being of one substance,
same substance
expressing

as love

Heaven

In the blue light of the Kingdom of Heaven
you no longer observe it streaming
from the window of God,
for you are that flood of light
illuminating the consciousness of all beings.

You no longer feel the love expressed by all life,
for you are that love bursting from the hearts of all creatures.

You no more sense the energy enlivening all sentient beings,
for you are that power arising in their souls.

Contained in stardust,
distilling the whole magnificence of the universe
you are that.

The Bee

A bee appears
hovering before her eyes
motionless on frantic wings
urgent, compelling;

"How do you do that?
Why are you there?"

Even before the question mark arises,
the reply:

"Because."

"What is the meaning of this?
What is your message?"

Quick as light the answer comes
in the knowing:

"Be cause."

So easily missed
in the hasty departure:

"Be Cause."

Water

I am the great cloud of unknowing
the great silence of God
as nebulous and formless as atmospheres
and I am in each formed raindrop
each precipitating as a soul to the parched earth,
the desert that I am.
Each tumbling from the sky scud
separated out and running
together in the gossiping swirl
the spilling on the mountain slide
the sinking into dark rock that I am.

I am the life of the river
The harmonious flux and flow
the soul of flow
the sweep and curve
the mighty force flooding out
into the stilling deep, the big sea sleep.

I am the baptismal descent
into the infinite ocean immense,
the crashing wave and lapping shore
the sparkling chop and change
the blow and bluster of glory,
immortal presence.

I am the silent invisible spirit rising
the letting go,
the taking up,
the melting moment of transience.

And I am the cloud
raining souls on earth
to find form following the old
carving the new

I am river
    I am ocean
        I am the vanishing
          I am cloud

Disappearance

When God disappears
take bread
re-member Him as Christ
in your own flesh.